# THE TREASURES OF THE UFFIZI

*Text by*
*Luisa Becherucci*

**GIUNTI**

Translated by Paula Boomsliter for Lexis

© 1998 Giunti Gruppo Editoriale, Florence
First edition: May 1998

| Reprint | | | | | | Year | | | | |
|---|---|---|---|---|---|---|---|---|---|---|
| 8 | 7 | 6 | 5 | 4 | 3 | | 2005 | 2004 | 2003 | 2002 |

Printed by Giunti Industrie Grafiche S.p.A. – Prato

The Galleria degli Uffizi originated as a repository for the art treasures amassed by the Medici family. Begun by Cosimo the Elder, at the suggestion, it would seem, of Donatello, and amplified by his sons Piero and Giovanni and his nephew Lorenzo II il Magnifico, the main scope of these collections was to acquire documents from that classical world which was the ideal model of all humanistic culture. But they also gave the contemporary world its due right from the beginning: Lorenzo's collections in the garden near San Marco comprised classical works as well as those of great Renaissance artists such as Donatello, Brunelleschi, Masaccio, Paolo Uccello, Fra Angelico and Filippo Lippi. Collecting was, however, not the wealthy Lorenzo's only passion: he also helped young artists by maintaining them at his expense and furthering their training by allowing them to study his treasures of art, which were in the custody of the sculptor Bertoldo, a pupil of Donatello. One of those young artists was Michelangelo.

The Medici collection thus laid the groundwork for the formation of the great modern institutions, although centuries were to pass before those premises became universally-accepted canons.

The superb collection was dispersed and damaged as a result of pillage by the populace and shrewd "appropriations" at the hands of the French when the Medici fled Florence after Charles

**CIMABUE** *THE VIRGIN WITH THE CHILD, ANGELS AND PROPHETS* (AND DETAIL)

VIII had invaded Italy (1494); part of the collection was recovered, but it was again pillaged during the stormy period of Medicean rule in the first decades of the sixteenth century. It was not until the days of Cosimo I, duke and later grand duke of Tuscany, that the collection was given what one might call a new beginning. Cosimo was anxious to revive the cultural traditions of his family and was an enthusiastic collector of gems, medals and sculptures; he commissioned Giorgio Vasari to plan a building for the offices (in Italian, *uffizi*) of the government judiciary and join it to the new Pitti palace by means of a corridor. In about 1581, Cosimo's eccentric son and heir, Francesco I, conceived the idea of assembling the already conspicuous Medici family collection in the loggia above the palace.

He called the assembled collection the *Galleria*, after the French, and the word was subsequently applied to other art collections all over the world. For Florence, it signified the coalescing of a grandiose cultural nucleus from which there branched out all the other artistic and scientific institutions that have made Florence a center of world culture over the centuries.

The portion of the Uffizi built under Francesco I can still be identified despite the subsequent additions. It comprised the east loggia, which was closed in at that time so as to form the first *corridore*; the octagonal Tribuna, designed by Buontalenti, provides access to various adjacent rooms.

The desire to celebrate both a great past and a present of which people were proudly conscious left its mark on the Galleria from the start, and has continued to determine its subsequent development down to our own times. Buontalenti placed statues in the long corridor, not only as examples of classical art but as richly decorative elements in candid relief amidst the lovely colors of the mannerist decoration. Along the top of the walls, like a frieze, were placed portraits of illustrious men of all times, copied by Cristofano dell'Altissimo from those of Paolo Giovio's famous collection in Como. The ceilings were decorated with a web of airy, many-colored grotesques painted by Alessandro Allori with the help of his pupils Lodovico Buti, Giovanni Balducci, Giovanni Maria Butteri, Giovanni Bizzelli and Alessandro Pieroni. According to Bocchi's 1591 description, the Tribuna had its walls covered with red velvet, in perfect chromatic accord with the blue of the upper frieze and the cupola, encrusted with delicate mother-of-pearl decorations designed by Poccetti. The Tribune contained the most precious things, such as Giambologna's statuettes of the *Labors of Hercules*, standing out against the velvet, and other small carvings in bronze, agate, jasper and turquoise. In the center, in a domed case – a beautiful work in rock crystal and hard stone - were the medals, cameos and cut gems. It must have looked like the glittering interior of a magic casket, containing as it did paintings such as Raphael's *Portrait of Leo X* and his *Madonna della Seggiola*, Andrea del Sarto's *Noblewoman* and Pontormo's *Charity*, all of which celebrated that climax of art that it seemed had been achieved in the Cinquecento. At the sides, in small rooms with ceilings likewise elaborately decorated, were collections of weapons from all countries, even from America, and also instruments used in the study of physics, which in those days had an artistic quality that has since been lost. It was, like his secluded Studiolo in Palazzo Vecchio, the realization of one of Francesco I's fantastic dreams. This restless desire for knowledge induced him – as Montaigne noted when he visited Italy in 1580 – to shut himself up in the laboratories of the "Casino" of San Marco, where he carried out all kinds of strange pseudoscientific and mechanical experiments: distilling medicaments and essences, making artificial imitations of hard stones, manufacturing porcelain, and producing strange works of goldsmithery. But the Galleria, which perhaps represents the ideal climax of his cultural eclecticism, was only begun by him. It was continued by his brother Ferdinand I, who succeeded him and who, while possessed of the same passion for beautiful things common to all the Medici, was endowed with a much more balanced mind. While still Cardinal, he collected in his Roman villa on the Pincio many classical marbles, such as *Venus* and the *Children of Niobe*, which much later were brought to Florence to enrich the collection there, for which he purchased, for example, Michelangelo's *Bacchus*. When in Florence, the new Galleria was the focus of his interests. In the Tribuna, which by that time had assumed the form described by Bocchi, he placed the well-known "diamond of Tuscany," that most bril-

**GIOTTO** *THE VIRGIN WITH THE CHILD AND ANGELS* (AND DETAIL)

liant of all gems, subsequently purloined by the Lorraine family. Pigafetta, in his comment on a song written for the wedding of Maria de' Medici and King Henry IV of France, celebrated this room as "inky-dark and studded with gold and silver and silk, like a heavenly dwelling and a star-spangled cloister." At that time the workshops, such as those for mosaics and tarsia work, subsequently to become the Opificio delle Pietre Dure, had already been transferred to the western end of the loggia, which terminated, on the terrace above the Loggia dei Lanzi, in a hanging garden "planted with evergreen trees and flowers for the delectation of the princely heir and his brothers, whither they are wont to go each day towards evening to hear the ordinary music of the palace above the piazza."

All the Medicean grand dukes were interested in the Galleria and made their contributions to it. Even the feeble and sickly Cosimo II, who placed in it Correggio's *Virgin in adoration*, presented to him by the Duke of Mantua in 1617. But Ferdinand II (1621-1670) left a far deeper mark. He had as his enthusiastic collaborator his brother, Cardinal Leopoldo (d. 1675), who had not only a taste for collecting but also a profound and refined culture. Times were changing: Galileo had founded the new scientific method, that ultimate fruit of Florentine civilization by now in its decline in the artistic field, and the Cardinal was a follower of the new studies, a friend of Galileo, and a framer, in 1657, of the Accademia del Cimento instituted by the grand duke in 1651. He collected many things, but his methods were very different from those of an eclectic amateur. Though a Florentine, he had a predilection for Venetian painting and he acquired some beautiful specimens with the aid of the antiquary Del Sera. His collections of drawings, miniatures and models, and painters' self-portraits were the more subtly discriminating continuation of Cosimo I's encyclopedic iconography, and with them he initiated those specialized collections which, as they grew, eventually gave rise to separate institutions. Ferdinand II entrusted him with the task of supervising the enlargement of the Galleria, already too small in relation to its contents. The additions consisted of the corridor toward the west and the adjacent rooms until then used as workshops. Decoration of the ceilings, which celebrated every aspect of Tuscan civilization, began in 1658 under the direction of the erudite Ferdinando Del Maestro and by the hands of Cosimo Ulivelli, Angelo Gori, Jacopo Chiavistelli, Giuseppe Masini and Giuseppe Tonelli. Soon the new rooms were ready to receive the works of art that flowed into the grand-ducal treasury. From the bequest of Don Antonio Medici, Prince of Capistrano, came the Mantegna triptych and other masterpieces. When the Della Rovere family, to which the grand duchess Vittoria belonged, died out in 1631, the grand dukes inherited many works of art, for example the *Portraits* of Federico da Montefeltro and Battista Sforza by Piero della Francesca, Raphael's *Self Portrait* and the *Portrait of Julius II* attributed to him, and a group of masterpieces by Titian: the *Venus* with the little dog and the two *Portraits* of Guidobaldo and Eleonora of Urbino.

The earlier enthusiasm for antiquity and especially for ancient sculpture was gradually replaced by interest in modern painting, as the classical ideals on which Renaissance civilization had been modeled lost ground. Even though Ferdinand II acquired some fine sculptures, such as the *Hermaphrodite* purchased from the Ludovisi family, and the *Idolino* of Pesaro that was part of the Della Rovere bequest, his principal additions were in the field of painting. The Galleria, though still known as "Gallery of Statues" to distinguish it from the Palatine "Quadreria" or picture-gallery which was then taking shape at Palazzo Pitti, began to assume its still-prevalent character as a collection of paintings. By 1635, Michelangelo's *Holy Family* was hung in the Tribuna, and in 1639 Correggio's *Rest on the Flight into Egypt* was acquired by exchange from the Duke of Modena.

Even the bigoted Cosimo III, who succeeded the enlightened Ferdinand II in 1670, left his cultural mark on the Galleria. It is probable, though not certain, that the acquisition of a late masterpiece by Rembrandt, the *Portrait of the Rabbi Morteira*, was the result of Cosimo's visit to Holland when he was still a young

**SIMONE MARTINI** *THE ANNUNCIATION*
(AND DETAIL)

15

**GENTILE DA FABRIANO** *THE ADORATION OF THE MAGI* (AND DETAILS)

17

man. Leonardo's *Adoration of the Magi* was moved to the Galleria in 1670, as were parts of Cardinal Leopoldo's collections when he died in 1675. Among these were the self-portraits, and in the same room in which they were hung the grand duke placed the statue of Leopoldo by Foggini. From the Villa Medici in Rome came the *Venus*, the *Grinder* and the *Wrestlers* that still adorn the Tribuna. At the same time the collection of medals was augmented by no less than 13,000 items. It is interesting to note that when a custodian of the collection of gems was appointed in the person of Sebastiano Bianchi, the grand duke provided for his training by sending him first to Bologna, then to Rome and finally on a tour of France before he took office.

Grand Prince Ferdinand had meanwhile assembled a collection of his own, often acquiring famous works from convents and churches. One of these was Andrea del Sarto's *Madonna with the Harpies*. Following the prince's death in 1713, these too were assigned to the Galleria. And finally, the fundamentally inept Gian Gastone, the last of the Medicean grand dukes, acquired a number of gems and antique inscriptions for the Galleria.

The Enlightenment was encroaching and with it a desire for critical review of the works that had been collected and for making them better known. It was during these years that Scipione Maffei paid frequent visits to the Galleria, which he examined with admiring but unprejudiced eyes, and for the first time expressed doubt as to the authenticity of certain antique items. The need for systematic study became more and more evident and the publication of the *Museo Fiorentino*, a grandiose work promoted by a committee of nobles under the presidency of Senator Filippo Buonarroti, was begun. The aim of the publication was to make known, by means of reproductions in the form of engravings accompanied by an appropriate commentary, all the works contained in Florentine collections, beginning with those in the Galleria. The opus, divided into various volumes according to subject, was published in instalments between 1731 and 1752. Meanwhile the Medici family had died out, with an act of sovereign, enlightened liberality. In 1737, Anna Maria Luisa, sister of Gian Gastone and wife of the Elector Palatine, made a "family agreement" (subsequently confirmed by her will in 1743) with the new grand duke, Francis I of Lorraine, whereby all the Medicean collections were bequeathed to the person of the prince "on the express condition that none of those works which are an ornament of the State, of utility to the public, and attract the curiosity of strangers, shall be transported away or removed from the Capital of the State of the Grand Duchy." And thus that which is held to be the greatest collection in the world became the "intangible patrimony" of Florence.

The age of Enlightenment was now triumphant. Francis I of Lorraine, being unable by virtue of the agreement to remove any of these beautiful works to Vienna, wished at least to have reproductions of them. Beginning in 1748, he commissioned a number of artists, under the supervision of P. De Greys, to make drawings of all the rooms of the Galleria, some of which are still in the Drawings and Prints Section annexed to the Uffizi. Copper engravings were also made of the ceilings in the second corridor. In 1759, Giuseppe Bianchi, at the time the chief custodian of the Galleria, printed his *Ragguaglio*, the first real catalogue of the collection. Then the cultural interests of the evolving times found their interpreter in the new grand duke, Pietro Leopoldo.

A new and fecund era thus began for the Galleria degli Uffizi, which began to be managed in accordance with modern ideas. Management was no longer a matter of simple numerical increase of the number of possessions, although all the collections were liberally augmented by the grand duke, who brought the statues of the *Children of Niobe* back from Rome, returned to the Galleria a number of works scattered among various State offices, such as the *Virtues* by Antonio del Pollaiolo and Fra

MASACCIO *ST. ANNE WITH THE VIRGIN AND CHILD* (AND DETAIL)

**PAOLO UCCELLO**
*THE BATTLE OF SAN ROMANO* (AND DETAIL)

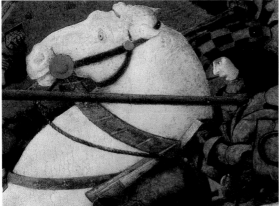

Angelico's *Madonna dei Linaioli*, and also acquired self-portraits, medals, Egyptian and Etruscan objects (in which scholars were becoming increasingly interested), and a magnificent example of Greek sculpture, the *Torso of a Faun*. There now arose the need to undertake systematic rearrangement of the immense number of

items accumulated over the course of centuries in rooms which were inevitably too small to contain them.

Those in charge of the Galleria at the time were men with broad, solid cultural backgrounds. In 1775, after the death of the erudite Raimondo Cocchi, Giuseppe Pelli was appointed to succeed him, with a great art historian, Luigi Lanzi, as his collaborator. In his valuable *Saggio istorico della Real Galleria di Firenze*, published in 1779, Pelli for the first time traced the history of the

**PIERO DELLA FRANCESCA** *PORTRAIT OF FEDERICO DA MONTEFELTRO*

PIERO DELLA FRANCESCA *TRIUMPH OF FEDERICO DA MONTEFELTRO*

Galleria from its beginnings, and Lanzi carried out the re-arrangement authorized by Pietro Leopoldo in 1780. Lanzi's organization of the Galleria collections followed a criterion of arrangement according to schools, including a comprehensive view of Italian painting in every century, the same criterion that informs his *Storia pittorica d'Italia*, a book of unquestioned value even today. In the course of the general rearrangement, which Pietro Leopoldo wished seen through as quickly as possible and which he himself supervised, all the material was subjected to

SANDRO BOTTICELLI *PRIMAVERA* (AND DETAIL)

critical selection. Many items were eliminated from the Galleria, for example the scientific instruments, which were sent to the new Cabinet of Physics, the collection of porcelain and, unfortunately, that of weapons, which was irretrievably dispersed. To the rooms thus made available he had others added, such as the delightful oval Cabinet of Gems, designed by Zanobi Rossi and decorated by Lucci, and the Niobe Room, designed by Gaspare Paoletti with elaborate decorations by Grato Albertolli, in which the statues of the children of Niobe provided an early impulse to the affirmation of the incipient neo-classical taste.

Some of the ceilings in the second corridor had been destroyed in a fire in 1762; they were restored or painted afresh by Giuseppe del Moro, Giuliano Traballesi and Giuseppe Terreni. The monumental new rooms formed a harmonious continuation of the sumptuous appearance that had marked the Galleria since its inception. The *gabinetti* ("cabinets" or exhibition rooms) off the corridors were increased in number from ten to twenty, and Pietro Leopoldo decreed that adjoining these there should be rooms for use as offices, in which all the documents of the Galleria's archives were to be stored, and a library containing books useful for the study of the various works. The scheme thus included every feature of a modern cultural center; and the grand duke ordered that it should be open to the public and drew up regulations for the safeguarding of the works and the hours of admission. In this way the Galleria, born from the aulic

HUGO VAN DER GOES *THE PORTINARI TRIPTYCH*
*(ADORATION OF THE SHEPHERDS WITH SAINTS AND THE DONORS PRAYING* AND DETAIL)

**ANDREA MANTEGNA** *THE CIRCUMCISION*
(DETAIL FROM *THE TRIPTYCH OF THE ADORATION OF THE MAGI AND THE ASCENSION* AND DETAILS)

GIOVANNI BELLINI *ALLEGORY*
(AND DETAIL)

culture of the princes, became an important cultural instrument for the populace. Archaeology, with all its specialized branches, and art history were gradually becoming independent sciences, and by the end of the eighteenth century the arrangement of the Galleria met the new needs quite comfortably. In many respects, the arrangement described by Lanzi in his volume *La Real Galleria di Firenze*, published in 1782, still holds good today. Although the Galleria at the time still contained both ancient and modern works, there was already a clear tendency towards a classification that was not merely chronological and topographical but also subject-oriented. The paintings of the German and

Flemish schools were already displayed in separate rooms. One room was reserved for what was later called "primitive" painting; that is, works of the fourteenth and fifteenth centuries, the majority Florentine, which the intervening centuries had neglected in the belief, perfectly aligned with the evolutionistic views that had prevailed since Vasari, that they were no more than imperfect preparatory sketches for the sixteenth-century apogee of the Renaissance

The drawings and prints were at this time collected in albums and arranged on shelves like books in libraries. In the Tribuna, from which the bronzes and gems had been removed to other

LEONARDO DA VINCI *THE ANNUNCIATION* (AND DETAIL)

rooms, remained the most highly prized works. In addition to the most notable sculptures – *Venus*, the *Grinder*, the *Wrestlers* and the *Dancing Faun* – it also contained the masterpieces of the Cinquecento, among them Michelangelo's *Tondo*, the *Madonna of the Goldfinch* and *St. John* by Raphael and the portrait of *Julius II* attributed to him, Correggio's *Madonna Worshiping the Child*, Parmigianino's *Holy Family* and Titian's recumbent *Venus*.

As interest extended beyond the Renaissance, there were added works by Guido Reni, Guercino, Lanfranco and Albani, artists of that seventeenth-century Bolognese school who seemed to continue the Renaissance ideals of formal election. Other paintings were hung on the long walls of the corridors. The entrance to the Galleria was placed where it still is, beyond the staircase built by Vasari for the Medicean theater, and was enhanced by the addition of an oval vestibule adorned with statues and classical reliefs.

When Pietro Leopoldo became Emperor Leopold II of Austria in 1790, the Galleria degli Uffizi remained as a fundamental monument of his enlightened government of Tuscany. His successor, Ferdinand III, had only to preserve it, but he too went beyond the minimum required of him and made many notable

**RAFFAELLO SANZIO** *THE MADONNA OF THE GOLDFINCH* (AND DETAIL)

MICHELANGELO BUONARROTI *THE HOLY FAMILY*

additions with an advantageous exchange of works negotiated with Vienna in 1793 which brought a whole series of master-pieces to the Galleria, including Titian's *Flora*, Giovanni Bellini's *Allegory*, and Dürer's *Adoration of the Magi*. The Venetian section, already conspicuous thanks to Cardinal Leopoldo's legacy, thus demanded a separate location. The task of providing one was undertaken by Tommaso Puccini, who had succeeded Pelli as curator in 1793. But the clouds of the Napoleonic wars were already massing and Puccini was forced to turn his energies to preserving the collections from the rapacious avidity of the French commissaries. This he did with zeal and tenacity, but not always with success. The *Medici Venus* and some of the most pre-cious gems were entrusted to the custody of the King of Naples and taken to Palermo. But in vain, for Ferdinand IV proved inca-pable of resisting the pressure brought to bear on him by the First Consul, and the *Venus* was for some time, so to say, exiled to Paris. It was followed, in 1810, by many other Tuscan masterpieces, only part of which were recovered after the fall of Napoleon.

With the return of peace, the Galleria continued on its proud course. But the progress and cultural evolution of the later years of the nineteenth century created new needs to which Lanzi's organization could no longer adequately respond except perhaps as regarded the general arrangement of the collections. The amount of material increased every year; the suppression of the monasteries resulted in the arrival of quantities of works in the store-rooms of the Accademia di Belle Arti and in the rooms of the former manastery of San Marco. Other works arrived from the excavations at Etruscan sites and as a result of the increasing interest in Egyptian antiquities. The modern thirst for knowledge continually demanded new material and better facilities for studying and classifying that material in accordance with the new categories into which science was being divided.

The great collections of the Galleria, originally assembled in order to provide a contrast between the two greatest periods in the story of mankind – classical antiquity and the Renaissance – had now to serve the very different research needs of modern science. And there began that phenomenon, typical of the life of the Galleria during the nineteenth century, of the creation of specialized institutions for material which the Uffizi building was no longer able to contain.

The first step in reorganization was to separate the archaeo-logical collections from the rest to give rise to the Egyptian Museum in the Cenacolo di Foligno; a few years later (1867), the Etruscan items were also moved there, and in 1870 the Archaeological Museum came into existence. Then it was the turn of the surviving weapons, of the maiolicas from Urbino, the bronzes and the modern sculptures, which in 1864, when Florence was the capital of the Kingdom of Italy, were trans-ferred to the new National Museum in the Bargello palace. The Galleria degli Uffizi was then cleared of everything not falling within the two categories of antique sculpture and painting. The former remained static, since new archaeological finds were sent to the museum designed for them; the latter was dynamic, sub-ject to continual and rapid growth, since Romantic thinking considered painting the highest expression of art and made it the subject of a new, rapidly developing branch of study – the histo-ry of art. And the Galleria, from the second half of the nineteenth century until World War II, reflected that thought in both its acquisitions and its organization.

The additions made during the last decades of the nineteenth century and the first of the twentieth consisted to a large extent of the "primitive" works of artists who lived before the Cinquecento, a period the history of which the critics of the time were enthusiastically reconstructing on new bases. Suppressed convents and churches supplied the Galleria with works such as Leonardo's early *Annunciation*, Domenico Veneziano's altar-piece

TIZIANO VECELLIO *FLORA*

of the *Madonna with Four Saints*, Lorenzo Monaco's *Coronation of the Virgin*, and Botticelli's *Annunciation*. When the capital of Italy was transferred from Florence to Rome, rooms to accommodate these and other masterpieces of the Tuscan school were found – under the guidance of the then Curator Enrico Ridolfi – in the hall of the Senate which had occupied the Medicean theater. Unfortunate though it may have been, the placement of the drawings in the corridor built by Vasari above the Ponte Vecchio, opened to the public in 1866, freed other rooms.

In 1900, the collection of paintings of the Arcispedale di Santa Maria Nuova was acquired, and among other works there came to the Galleria the great triptych by Hugo van der Goes. A Rubens room was also inaugurated with the two huge canvases formerly hung in the Niobe room.

At this point of its chaotic expansion, the Galleria degli Uffizi had the great good fortune to be entrusted, in 1903, to the curatorship of Corrado Ricci, who in the course of only three years drew up the plan for its definitive reorganization. In the spaces provided by the former Medicean theater, on the first floor, he founded the Cabinet of Drawings and Prints for the valuable graphics collection which had previously been exposed to deleterious influences in Vasari's Corridor, where he instead placed the iconographic collections. He also organized a special group of rooms for the collection of self-portraits, which was continually increasing. He restored the Loggia of Geographical Maps by enclosing it with glass, and in it he placed Piero della Francesca's two portraits. In accordance with his conception of the Galleria as a center for the study of art history, he added reading rooms and a photographic archive to the library, which he moved to rooms suitable for responding to its needs for expansion. Lastly, it was his idea that the whole of the Uffizi palace, once freed from the State Archives that occupied the first floor, should become the home of other museums (Ricci was thinking of the

ANTONIO ALLEGRI CALLED IL CORREGGIO
*THE VIRGIN ADORING THE CHILD*

FRANCESCO MAZZOLA CALLED IL PARMIGIANINO
*THE MADONNA WITH THE CHILD AND ST. ZACHARIAS* (AND DETAIL)

Archaeological Museum in particular) so as to form a complex similar to those which were being created in other countries.

The program sketched out by Ricci was implamented out by his successors, though with certain modifications. In the years that followed, despite the interruption of the work caused by World War I (1915-18) and the consequent dispersal of the works of art, Giovanni Poggi, assisted by Nello Tarchiani, was

able to bring the Galleria to the highest possible level of efficiency from the artistic and historical points of view.

Reading the catalogue edited by Giovanni Poggi in 1926, one is surprised at the enormous number of works that entered the Uffizi as a result of the rearrangement after the war, most of them from the crowded galleries of the Accademia. The aim was to integrate every section of the Galleria, but special attention was paid to the period between the end of the thirteenth and the sixteenth centuries, the most glorious phase of Florentine painting. The ensemble thus brought together had no rival anywhere. Cimabue and Giotto were represented by the grandiose *Madonna*s from Santa Trinita and the Ognissanti church, and around them were works of the Florentine school (Bernardo Daddi, Taddeo Gaddi, Orcagna) and those of the other pole of Italian civilization at the time – the Sienese school. Simone Martini's *Annunciation*, which had been in the Galleria since the eighteenth century, was flanked by paintings by Pietro and Ambrogio Lorenzetti (*Blessed Humility*, the *Presentation in the Temple, Stories from the Life of St. Nicholas*). The works of Lorenzo Monaco now staad side by side with Gentile da Fabriano's *Adoration of the Magi*, thus evoking the Late Gothic current in which the impending Renaissance was already a palpable presence. And Masaccio's *St. Anne* was there to mark the full affirmation of the Renaissance. To the panels by Paolo Uccello, Domenico Veneziano, and Antonio del Pollaiolo were added the group of works by Filippo Lippi. The whole complex was admirably integrated with Botticelli's *Primavera*, which now hung close to his *Birth of Venus*, the *Madonna with Saints*, and the *Pallas and the Centaur*.

The completion of this Renaissance section alone would have sufficed to make the Galleria degli Uffizi "unique" among the great art collections of the world. But every other section had been augmented in like manner. About 1922, in the midst of the enthusiasm for the study of Baroque painting that led to a criti-

MICHELANGELO MERISI CALLED IL CARAVAGGIO
*BACCHUS*

cal reconsideration of those two neglected centuries, the seventeenth and eighteenth, the Galleria was enriched by sections devoted to them. It was about this time that Matteo Marangoni and Roberto Longhi identified Caravaggio's *Young Bacchus*, long forgotten in the store-rooms of the Uffizi. And while since the beginning of this century works by Tiepolo, Canaletto and Guardi had been acquired, there had also been removed from the store-rooms and exhibited almost-forgotten works by artists who art criticism was gradually rediscovering, such as Cavallino, Strozzi, Magnasco and Giuseppe Maria Crespi.

The Galleria by then possessed examples of every period of Italian painting and a vast selection of works of foreign schools. Chronological and topographical arrangement criteria were followed except in the Tribuna, which contained works of the more court-oriented Cinquecento together with portraits of the Medici by Pontormo, Bronzino and Vasari. The result was a living synthesis of history, in line with that which art historians had built up through a century of assiduous philological analysis. The new rooms no longer sought to emulate the sumptuousness of the granducal gallery; they were simple and unadorned, and well-lighted, so that every picture could be easily studied and compared, scientific study then having surpassed aesthetic contemplation of the works in importance.

This state of things was abruptly interrupted by World War II (1940-45). While the works of art were evacuated, removed to shelters or in some cases subjected to long journeys across the Alps, the destruction by explosives of streets and bridges in the center of Florence, in the immediate vicinity of the Uffizi, caused grievous damage to the building. Owing to explosions, the admirable frescoed ceilings were on the point of collapsing or crumbling to pieces. It took all the tenacity Giovanni Poggi was able to muster, and that of his second-in-command Filippo Rossi, to undertake and to carry through to conclusion the

PETER PAUL RUBENS
*PORTRAIT OF ISABELLA BRANDT*

51

immense and delicate work of restoration that was begun immediately after the end of the war and which to an almost incredible degree succeeded in restoring the building to its traditional appearance.

But the war damage did not extend to the buildings alone. In that violent upset of all that had been produced in a slow, centuries-long process, many problems had suddenly come to a head, and a rapid completion of the restoration in progress became imperative. The Superintendents Filippo Rossi and Guglielmo Pacchini, in their work of rearranging the Uffizi, had to face the problem of satisfying contemporary demands with a structure which had inevitably aged. Despite economic and other difficulties, and assisted by the curator of the Galleria, Roberto Salvini, and by the architects Lando Bartoli and Guido Morozzi, they managed to cope with the task. Heating, air-conditioning and lighting systems were renovated or new ones installed; there was also the no less demanding problem of how to arrange the works in the restored rooms, to which it had been possible to add another large hall. Chronological or topographical sequence now seemed insufficient in light of the studies being produced in scientific and scholarly circles.

The present-day arrangement of the Uffizi Gallery - awaiting the overall restructuring to come with the creation of the so-called "Grandi Uffizi" - has been inevitably influenced by this state of affairs. If certain steps have won universal approval, such as that of reserving the new hall for a general comparison between the Florentine and the Flemish Renaissance, and two other rooms for the Mannerists to whom recent criticism has restored their rightful historic value, others have been the cause of controversy and criticism.

The most recent episode in the enhancement of the collection dates to 1989, when under the direction of Annamaria Petrioli Tofani (who succeeded Luciano Berti), a hundred or so

REMBRANDT VAN RIJN
*YOUTHFUL SELF-PORTRAIT*

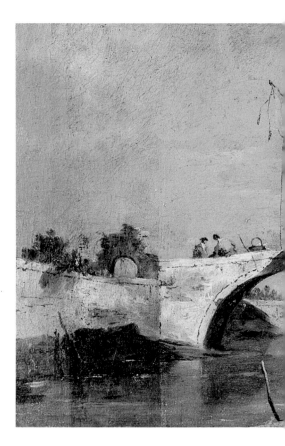

FRANCESCO GUARDI
*VIEW OF A CANAL*

pieces, paintings and ancient sculptures, were acquired. They were those recovered by Rofolfo Siviero, the plenipotentiary who on behalf of the Italian government dedicated a large part of his life to searching for the works stolen by the Nazi Germans during the last war. Among others, the *Leda* of Leonardo's school. Other new additions have emerged after careful examination of the material preserved in the store-rooms, and much has also been accomplished in the field of restoration (for example, the

three *Maestà* by Duccio, Cimabue and Giotto).

The latest episode in the history of the Galleria degli Uffizi, unfortunately, was reported on the crime news pages worldwide. On 27 May 1993 a bomb - which investigation revealed to be linked to a Mafia-supported terrorist strategy - exploded in Via dei Georgofili under the western wing of the building. It produced enormous damage in terms both of loss of human life and of damage to Italy's cultural heritage. Fifty or so paintings and

FRANCESCO GUARDI
*VIEW OF A CANAL* (DETAIL)

sculptures suffered more or less serious injury. Most of the damaged works have been restored, but three will never again be displayed: the *Adoration of the Shepherds* by Gherardo delle Notti and Bartolomeo Manfredi's *Concert* and the *Card Players*.

# CAPTIONS
# TO THE ILLUSTRATIONS

**CIMABUE** (Florence, known to have been active from 1272 to 1303)
*THE VIRGIN WITH THE CHILD, ANGELS AND PROPHETS*

p.6

Painted for the high altar of the church of Santa Trinita in Florence. From 1810 in the Accademia di Belle Arti; since 1919 in the Uffizi. The vigor of the draftsmanship, which engraves and molds the severe countenances, is a proof of the new, dramatic power that Cimabue, even in the early days before his great works in Assisi, was capable of giving to the models influenced by Byzantine art that inspired his work.

**GIOTTO** (Vespignano in Mugello 1267? - Florence 1337)
*THE VIRGIN WITH THE CHILD AND ANGELS*

p.10

Painted for the church of Ognissanti in Florence. From 1810 in the Accademia di Belle Arti; since 1919 in the Uffizi. A work of Giotto's late mature period, painted about 1310, in which the conquest of form is fully achieved by gradations of light on the planes of the figures which seem to stand in statuary relief; the figuration is ideally heightened until it becomes sublime poetry in the ecstatic and radiant gaze of the Child and in the devout prayer of the Angels.

**SIMONE MARTINI** (Siena - Avignon 1344)
*THE ANNUNCIATION*

p.14

Signed and dated 1333; painted for the Sant'Ansano chapel in the Siena Cathedral by Martini with the collaboration, as regards the Saints at the sides, of Lippo Memmi. Since 1799 in the Uffizi. In this late work by the Sienese artist, the melodiousness of late Gothic art is carried to a supreme conclusion, giving a charming lyricism to the composition of the figures.

**GENTILE DA FABRIANO** (Fabriano 1360 - Rome, about 1427)
*THE ADORATION OF THE MAGI*

p.16

Signed and dated 1423. Painted for the Palla Strozzi chapel in the sacristy of Santa Trinita. Transferred to the Accademia di Belle Arti in 1810; since 1919 in the Uffizi. The delicate sense of life, which the late Gothic artists contemplated in all the beauty of its multiple aspects, finds a profound interpreter in Gentile, who tells us the story of the journey of the Magi as if it were a fairy-tale.

**MASACCIO** (San Giovanni Valdarno 1401 - Rome 1428)
*ST. ANNE WITH THE VIRGIN AND CHILD*

Painted for the church of Sant'Ambrogio in Florence, whence
it passed to the Accademia di Belle Arti and, in 1919, to the
Uffizi. This early work heralds the new, profoundly human art
introduced by Masaccio. It was probably painted about 1420,
with the collaboration, in a strictly subordinate sense,
of Masolino. The moral certitude of the figures, especially
that of the dignified Madonna, is expressed in the ample forms
revealed by the lighting in all their pure plastic essence.

p. 20

**PAOLO UCCELLO** (Pratovecchio 1397 - Florence 1475)
*THE BATTLE OF SAN ROMANO*

Originally in the "Chamber of Lorenzo" in the Medici palace in
Florence, where it formed the center panel of a triptych (the
other panels are now at the Louvre and the National Gallery,
London) of the victory of the Florentines over the Sienese at
San Romano in 1432. The panels were probably painted in
1456, as part of the posthumous tribute to the victorious
leader Niccolò da Tolentino. Men, animals and things, though
becoming the elements of an elaborate perspective scheme,
are transfigured in that unreal, highly pictorial manner peculiar
to the Gothic taste that persisted in this artist's work despite
his Renaissance intellectualism.

p. 22

**DOMENICO VENEZIANO** (Venice, mentioned 1438 - Florence 1461)
*THE MADONNA WITH THE CHILD AND FOUR SAINTS*

Formerly on the high altar in the Church of Santa Lucia de'
Magnoli in Florence. Since 1862 in the Uffizi. The painting can
be dated about 1445. The delicate chromatic construction
of this altar-piece is completely pervaded by the bright, almost
motionless light that creates for the tranquil religious devotion
of the Saints an atmosphere often found in Venetian painting.

p. 24

**PIERO DELLA FRANCESCA** (Sansepolcro 1416 - 1492)
*PORTRAIT OF FEDERICO DA MONTEFELTRO*

Together with that of his wife, Battista Sforza, this portrait of
the Duke of Urbino became the property of the Grand Dukes
of Tuscany in 1631, as part of the Della Rovere bequest. Both
portraits passed to the Uffizi in 1773. The two panels were
painted in 1465-66. The profile stands out against a sweeping
background bathed in light. In the allegory painted on the back
the solemn, motionless forms are permeated with the intense
luminosity that pours from the sky and is mirrored in the water.

p. 26

**SANDRO BOTTICELLI** (Florence 1445 - 1510)
*PRIMAVERA*

p. 28

Painted for the Villa of Castello, near Florence, at the time property of Lorenzo di Pierfrancesco de' Medici. The painting was transferred from the grand-ducal wardrobe to the Accademia di Belle Arti in 1853 and since 1919 has been in the Uffizi. May be dated about 1477-78. The subject has been given various interpretations besides the traditional one of an allegory of Spring: a representation of the kingdom of Venus (who appears at the center below a cherub), a representation of the cycle of the seasons, and others. The central figure would seem to represent Venus, with at her right Zephyr pursuing Flora to transform her into the spring breeze (with the flowered robe), and at her left Mercury with the three Graces.

**HUGO VAN DER GOES** (Gand ?, about 1435 - Soignies 1482)
*THE PORTINARI TRIPTYCH*
*ADORATION OF THE SHEPHERDS WITH SAINTS AND THE DONORS PRAYING*

p. 30

Formerly on the high altar of the church of Sant'Egidio. Painted at Bruges about 1476 for Tommaso Portinari, agent of the Medici, who sent it to Florence. Subsequently in the art gallery of the Arcispedale di Santa Maria Nuova, to which the church belonged. Purchased by the Uffizi in 1900. In the rediscovery of the real nature of things, carried out with a perfect mastery of the pictorial art, Flemish painting transformed its language based on Gothic models into Renaissance art. The stupendous still life forming the foreground of this masterpiece by Van der Goes is a most striking example of this process.

**ANDREA MANTEGNA**
(Isola di Cartura, Vicenza 1431 - Mantua 1506)
*THE CIRCUMCISION* (detail from the triptych of
*THE ADORATION OF THE MAGI AND THE ASCENSION*)

p. 32

The triptych was bequeathed to the Grand Dukes in 1632 by Don Antonio Medici, prince of Capistrano. It was then broken up into three parts; the Adoration was attributed to Botticelli. It was reassembled in 1827. Probably painted about 1464 for the chapel of the castle in Mantua. With Mantegna, who had studied the works of Donatello in Padua, the Florentine mastery of space, form and movement penetrates as an invigorating element into Venetian painting, paving the way for the innovations of Giambellino and Giorgione. In this work of Mantegna's early maturity, the line follows the dynamic tenseness of Donatello's draftsmanship, but the figures have a classical solidity, while the coloring of this heir of the Venetian Gothic school loses nothing of its fresh clarity.

**GIOVANNI BELLINI** (Venice after 1430 - 1516)
*ALLEGORY*

Since 1793 in the Uffizi, as a result of an exchange of pictures
with the Imperial Gallery in Vienna. The painting was a pretext,
for the mature Bellini, for creating a subtly lyrical evocation
of a twilight landscape, in which the densely-colored water,
houses and rocks are bathed in a motionless golden light
and the figures, placidly absorbed in their occupations, are
distributed in the vast space in such a way as to form
rhythmical interruptions without disturbing the sense of ecstatic
peacefulness. As to the subject, interpretations vary from
an allegory of Justice and Charity to a depiction of Paradise.

p. 35

**LEONARDO DA VINCI** (Vinci 1452 - Amboise 1519)
*THE ANNUNCIATION*

Since 1862 in the Uffizi. This is an early work of Leonardo,
who places the two figures in a spatial plane reminiscent
of Piero della Francesca in its vastness, attenuating by the
immobility of the composition the vibration of the light, which
shines intensely on every fold, on every veil and on every blade
of grass until it loses itself in an ethereal haze beyond the dark
curtain of the trees, in the receding marine landscape.
The picture is a stupendous prelude to the cosmic vibrations
of his later "sfumato".

p. 36

**RAFFAELLO SANZIO** (Urbino 1486 - Rome 1520)
*THE MADONNA OF THE GOLDFINCH*

Painted for Lorenzo Nasi of Florence about 1506. It appears
in the Uffizi inventory of 1708 and since the end of the
eighteenth century has been in the Tribuna. This is one
of Raphael's early works. During his stay in Florence between
1504 and 1506, he greatly admired the art of Leonardo,
from whom he took the harmonious structure of the
pyramidal composition, bathed in infinite vibrations of light.
This lighting, however, dissolves almost every shadow and
penetrates his warm, dense coloring reminiscent of Perugia
to unite in lyrical synthesis the gently dreaming figures
and the distant landscape beyond the little trees.

p. 38

61

### MICHELANGELO BUONARROTI
(Caprese 1475 - Rome 1564)
*THE HOLY FAMILY*

p. 40

This tondo was painted by Michelangelo about 1506 for Agnolo Doni. In 1635 it was already in the Tribuna at the Uffizi. The young Michelangelo's enthusiasm for grandiose form, clear despite the tense dynamic quality of his masses, is evident in this complicated group, born of the fantasy of a genius who had already personally relived every source of inspiration. Within the incisive drawing, the marble-like coloring is struck by the light as if by an exasperated chisel. But the nudes standing in the background, in a kind of invincible weariness, suggest the latent energy of form only by a sudden juxtaposition of lights and shades, a prelude to Michelangelo's later "non finito".

### TIZIANO VECELLIO
(Pieve di Cadore 1477 or 1490? - Venice 1576)
*FLORA*

p. 43

In the early seventeenth century this painting belonged to Don Alfonso Lopez, Spanish ambassador in Amsterdam. It then passed to the collection of Archduke Leopold Wilhelm, later to the Imperial Gallery in Vienna and finally to the Uffizi in 1793. The painting dates from Titian's early mature period, when he was adding accents of more resonant and passionate poetry to the undefined dreams of his master Giorgione. In the warm intensity of the chromatic tones, the youthful figure seems to bloom with intense life.

### ANTONIO ALLEGRI CALLED IL CORREGGIO
(Correggio, about 1489-1534)
*THE VIRGIN ADORING THE CHILD*

p. 45

This work can be dated between 1518 and 1520 and thus belongs to the artist's early mature period. In it he interprets the chiaroscuro contrasts of Leonardo's Lombard works in the gentle play of the light on the walls of the hut, on the trunk of the column and on the fragile hands stretching out towards the Child in timid adoration.

### FRANCESCO MAZZOLA CALLED IL PARMIGIANINO
(Parma 1503 - Casalmaggiore 1540)
*THE MADONNA WITH THE CHILD AND ST. ZACHARIAS*

p. 46

Since 1605 in the Tribuna at the Uffizi. Painted between 1527 and 1533 for Bonifazio Gozzadini of Bologna. Here Parmigianino's refined intellectualism, which he had absorbed in his youth in Rome, transforms Correggio's luminous grace into an elegant and subtle styling that earned Parmigianino a front-rank place among the creators of sixteenth-century mannerism.

**MICHELANGELO MERISI CALLED IL CARAVAGGIO**
(Caravaggio 1573 - Port'Ercole near Grosseto 1610)
*BACCHUS*

After being long forgotten in the store-rooms of the Uffizi, this
painting was identified by Matteo Marangoni and Roberto
Longhi, and since 1925 has been shown in the Uffizi Gallery. It
was probably painted about 1589 and is one of the works of
the artist's youth, permeated with his early enthusiasm for the
chromatic reality of things; in it, form overcomes the
conventions of the prevalent mannerist style to achieve a
vigorous harmony reminiscent almost of Raphael. The basket of
fruit, painted with an admirable feeling for values not yet
attenuated by the later interest in lighting, is one of the highest
achievements of Italian seventeenth-century painting.

p. 49

**PETER PAUL RUBENS** (Siegen 1577 - Antwerp 1640)
*PORTRAIT OF ISABELLA BRANDT*

This portrait came to the Uffizi in 1773 from the Villa Poggio
a Caiano. Isabella Brandt, Rubens' first wife, died in 1626.
This portrait is generally dated about 1620, at a time when the
artist, though comparatively young, was already in full
possession of his brilliant mastery of color: Here, he uses it
with rapid and flowing strokes of the brush to render the
vivacity of the young woman and the rich fabric of her clothing.

p. 51

**REMBRANDT VAN RIJN** (Leiden 1606 - Amsterdam 1669)
*YOUTHFUL SELF-PORTRAIT*

Known to have been in Marchese Gerini's collection in
Florence in 1724, the painting was purchased in 1818 by Grand
Duke Ferdinand III for the Galleria collection of self-portraits.
The theme of all Rembrandt's paintings is light, which reveals
images amidst mysterious darkness. But in this early work,
dated around 1634, the light spreads like a halo round the face,
clearly set off by its pale coloring, and envelops it in reflections
and spakkes on the iron gorget, on the red velvet and on the
golden necklet.

p. 53

**FRANCESCO GUARDI** (Venice 1712 - 1793)
*VIEW OF A CANAL*

Purchased for the Uffizi in 1905.
The painting belongs to Guardi's late period, during which
added lyricism to the prevailing objectivity in Venetian veduta
painting genre, evoking with light brushwork a lonely corner of
the cit, where the waters of the canal stagnate silently beneath
the bridges and reflect a greyish-blue sky, against which a pale
pink flag waves slowly.

p. 54/55

❖